HAWAIIAN RAILWAY

VOLUME 3 -- PLANTATION RAILWAYS ON OAHU

WWII PHOTOGRAPHS BY WWII SERVICEMEN:
VICTOR NORTON, JR., BILL BLEWETT, BOB ZINSMEISTER,
GRANT OAKES, JR., KENT COCHRANE AND VITALY UZOFF

WRITTEN BY GALE E. TREIBER

To all the World War II servicemen
who photographed and preserved railroad scenes in Hawaii
so that we can enjoy them today.

TABLE OF CONTENTS

FRONT COVER: The crew of Oahu Sugar Company #6, a Baldwin 0-6-2T named *Koalipea*, receives instructions from the supervisor in the broad-brimmed hat before returning to work. Photo by Victor Norton, Jr., Hawaiian Railway Society Collection.

REAR COVER MAIN PHOTO: *Ewa*, an 0-4-2T built by Baldwin in 1890, was Ewa Plantation's first locomotive. This beautiful portrait was taken by the U.S. Marine Corps' Bill Blewett, who was stationed at the nearby Ewa Marine Corps Air Station until shortly before the War's end.

Printed with pride
in the U.S.A.

The Railroad Press
PO Box 444
Hanover, PA 17331-0444

Printed in the United States of America.

International Standard Book Number 978-1-9314-7721-3

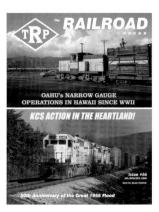

Publishers of:

TRP Magazine

*PRR Lines West
Pittsburgh to St. Louis
1960-1999*

*Illinois Central:
North of the Ohio River*

ALCO's to Allentown

Altoona Action

*Passenger Cars of
New England*

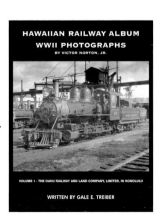

INTRODUCTION

ABOVE: Ewa Plantation #1, an 0-4-2T tank engine with a home-made tender for extra water capacity, was typical of Hawaii's early plantation locomotives. Photo by Bill Blewett.

Those of you who have purchased one of the earlier volumes in this Hawaiian Railway Album series have already learned the story of Victor Norton, Jr., a Sailor and railfan stationed at Pearl Harbor on the island of Oahu during World War II. His work schedule at the Ship Repair Unit allowed him enough liberty time to explore the island and visit most of its railways. These included the Oahu Railway and Land Company, covered in Volumes 1 and 2, plus five of the seven sugar plantation railways still intact at the end of the War. Victor also visited two of the other islands in the Hawaiian chain before he returned to the Mainland to muster out of the Navy. In May of 1945 he used his annual leave to visit Hawaii, the "Big Island," where he rode and photographed the Hawaii Consolidated Railway, which was covered in Volume 2. In March of 1946, just before he returned home, Victor visited Kauai. Kauai at that time still had five sugar plantations with operating railways, and Victor managed to not only visit each of them, but also to photograph most of their locomotives. His sugar cane railway photos form the basis for Volumes 3 and 4.

When I started assembling this volume, it became obvious that although Victor had done a very thorough job covering the Kauai plantations, his coverage of Oahu was not so complete. Photography restrictions during the War, plus the difficulty traveling to some of the outlying plantations, reduced his access to several of them. This meant that this third volume in the series would not have presented a complete picture of Oahu's plantations during and immediately after WWII unless another photographic collection could be found. When I presented this problem to the Hawaiian Railway Society's Historian Emeritus, Bob Paoa, he immediately put me in contact with Bill Blewett, another serviceman railfan who had spent most of the War years here on Oahu. Bill, a longtime member of the Hawaiian Railway Society, was quite willing to let the Society use his negatives for this book.

Bill Blewett started his working career on the Great Northern Railroad in 1941. Shortly after the attack on Pearl Harbor he entered the Marine Corps, and after completing bootcamp was assigned as a Military Policeman at the Marine Corps Air Station at

Ewa. Bill immediately discovered the OR&L, which ran right outside the airfield gate. Whereas Victor, prior to the end of the War, confined his rail photography to the limits of OR&L's yard at Iwilei, Bill, as an MP, apparently had a much easier time than Victor taking photographs out and around Oahu. Even though he returned to the Mainland in mid-1945, he had by then amassed an excellent collection of OR&L scenes both in and beyond Iwilei; and, more importantly for this volume, he had also photographed equipment at all seven of Oahu's plantations using his postcard format camera with 616 size film. After the War Bill returned to his native Minnesota, where he got a job as a motorman for the Minneapolis Street

Railway Company. When that line converted to busses in 1951, Bill headed south to the Chicago, South Shore and South Bend Railway, where he continued his vocation as a motorman for the rest of his working career. Bill currently resides in LaPorte, Indiana.

Another serviceman who passed through Hawaii shortly after the beginning of the War, courtesy of the U.S. Army, was Grant Oakes, Jr., of Wauwatosa, Wisconsin, who was temporarily stationed on Oahu during the May-July 1942 timeframe and, as shown later in this volume, spent what must have been a wonderful day photographing and riding one of Oahu's cane railways. And then there is Bob Zinsmeister of Braddock, Pennsylvania, who was stationed as a dark-

ABOVE: U.S. Army's Bob Zinsmeister poses at the controls of OR&L's motorcar M1 in Oahu's Iwilei Yard on the 17th of June in 1945, shortly before the end of the War in the Pacific. Bob served on Oahu with the U.S. Army Chemical Corps from 1943 through 1945. Collection of Bob Zinsmeister.

RIGHT: Bill Blewett spent three years on Oahu, serving as an MP at Marine Corps Air Station, Ewa. Here he is in Iwilei, near downtown Honolulu, posed on the footboard of OR&L 4-6-0 #88. Collection of Bill Blewett.

room technician with the Army Chemical Corps detachment at Schofield Barracks. Bob was another railfan that ventured off base to photograph Hawaii's railroads, getting around by either hitch-hiking or catching rides on military trucks. Although most of his 616 size photographs were taken on his monthly visits to the OR&L in Honolulu or on his two trips to the Hawaii Consolidated on the "Big Island" -- including his ride from Hilo to Paauilo on one of HCR's railbuses -- he did manage to take a few shots of locomotives on both the Ewa and Oahu Sugar plantations, and he graciously allowed us to use them in this volume.

However, even using these four collections, there were still rather significant gaps in Oahu's plantation railroad picture. Fortunately, Victor, after the War, traded for or purchased high quality photographic prints to complete his Hawaiian Railway photo collection. Scenes photographed shortly before or right after the end of WWII by Vitaly Uzoff, U.S. Army Signal Corps, and Kent Cochrane, U.S. Coast Guard -- unfortunately both now deceased -- filled in almost all of the remaining gaps, and they are presented here with the others to give as complete a picture as possible of Oahu's plantation railways and their equipment right around the end of the War.

We are indeed fortunate that the servicemen did not confine their railfanning to the busy OR&L main line, but that they left that better known beaten path to seek out the little lines and locomotives covered by this book. The majority of the plantation lines were still 100% steam at the time, which was certainly a draw, but the locomotives were quite small, most weighing between twenty and thirty tons, and for the most part were slow moving tank engines built to haul fifty or so loaded four or five-ton cane cars from the cane fields to the sugar mill at about fifteen miles per hour. They were simple machines, made for the self-sufficient shops found at each of the plantations. This was definitely not big-time railroading like these rail photographers had known back on the Mainland, and these industrial locomotives quite possibly would not have been worth a second look had there been more main-line variety. However, railfans, being railfans, tend to enjoy whatever is available. Now however, with all the plantation railways (and, as a matter of fact, all but two of Hawaii's sugar plantations) gone, these pictures preserve a way of life that has passed into history. As I noted earlier, we are indeed fortunate that these railfan photographers documented as much as they did.

Although not a WWII photographer, there is one more individual that deserves a huge amount of gratitude for preserving Hawaii's railroad history. Jesse Conde, a flight engineer for United Airlines on the Los Angeles-Honolulu route in the 1960's, spent his downtime here in the Islands researching Hawaii's plantation railway systems. He searched through old newspaper volumes, plantation corporate files plus those of the Sugar Planters Association, as well as locomotive and car builders' records, and he conducted personal interviews with those with first-hand experiences of these lines. His many years of effort resulted in what will almost certainly remain as the ultimate history of Hawaii's little industrial lines -- his 1973 book titled *Sugar Trains*. I used it as the principal reference for most of the historical background information and rosters found in this volume, and even though *Sugar Trains* is long out of print, I would recommend it highly to anyone who chooses to seriously study these little systems.

As an aside, many of you who have read the previous volumes of this series may recall that our original plan was to present an overview of Hawaii's railways just after WWII in a three volume set, with this third book covering all of Hawaii's sugar plantation railways. However, after we had finished gathering the photographs for Volume 3, we found that we had obtained so many exceptional and previously unpublished scenes here on Oahu that it would be better to share as many of them as we could and hold the photographs and information on Kauai and Hawaii's other islands for a fourth and final volume. We trust that you will find our presenting this more complete coverage the correct decision.

Once again I would like to thank the team that has worked on the first three books in this series: Hawaiian Railway Society for backing this project, their Historian Emeritus, Bob Paoa, for his historic and technical expertise, Gordon Ng of Honolulu's Colorprints for his skillful development of the photographs found in these books, John Treiber for his help with the maps, my wonderful wife, Georgia, for her patience and understanding when I spend too much time at the computer and forget to come down for dinner, and finally to our publisher, Jaime Serensits, for his encouragement, his wonderful efforts in removing flaws in our old negatives and for doing such a nice job in rearranging my manuscript and photos into these finished volumes. So, again, thanks to all of you!

Gale E. Treiber
Kapolei, Hawaii
July 2005

OAHU SUGAR RAILWAYS

From the time of the Oahu Railway and Land Company's inception products of Oahu's sugar plantations were its principal source of revenue. By the time the railroad reached its terminus at Kahuku in 1899, it had tied six of Oahu's seven major sugar mills to the port of Honolulu. However, at the end of World War II, after its heroic war effort, the OR&L's physical plant was worn out. Old steam locomotives needed to be replaced, and the roadbed, rails and bridges required major renovation. Railroad president Walter Dillingham met with the heads of the on-line plantations and presented his plan for rebuilding the OR&L -- contingent upon their acceptance of rate hikes for the transportation of sugar products. So great was their portion of OR&L traffic that when they refused,

he had no choice but to abandon the major portion of the railroad.

The map on the inside front cover shows the location of Oahu's sugar mills and most of the permanent trackage of the plantation railways that supplied sugar cane stalks to the mills. Like the OR&L big changes would soon be coming to their systems. Before the end of the War one of them, the Waimanalo Plantation Company, had abandoned its plantation railway. The railway systems of the other six, located on the OR&L in the following order from Honolulu -- Honolulu Plantation in Aiea, Oahu Sugar in Waipahu, Ewa Plantation in Ewa, Waianae Plantation in Waianae, Waialua Agricultural in Waialua and Kahuku Plantation in Kahuku -- would soon follow.

ABOVE: This is 0-6-2T #5, *Manana*, built by Baldwin in 1916 for the Honolulu Plantation Company with 33-inch drivers and 11x16-inch cylinders. This photograph is dated February 1946, well after Honolulu Plantation had substituted trucks for hauling cane from its fields. However, it shows *Manana* still under steam on a trestle near HPC's Aiea mill. Photo by Vitaly Uzoff. Collection of Victor Norton, Jr.

Prior to the end of WWII each of the principal plantations on Oahu had a permanent main line to bring sugar cane stalks from the fields to the mill. However, to minimize the total amount of track needed, each one also depended on a system of portable track that would be temporarily laid into each field that was ready for harvesting to get the small (4-5 ton capacity) cane cars as close as possible to the cut cane. Each of these portable track sections was about twenty-feet long and weighed as much as 160 pounds -- about as much as four strong men could carry. A dozen or so sections were moved on individual small flatcars to a switch at the entrance to each field, where a temporary railway roadbed would be made. A team of mules, later replaced by a caterpillar tractor, pulled these flatcars further and further along the temporary track as the rail sections were lifted off, carried ahead and snapped into place. When the track was ready a plantation locomotive would bring a string of cane cars from the mill to the junction with the very light portable track. There mules or a tractor would take over and pull short trains of empty cars out into the field, and, after they were loaded, return them to the railhead were they would be assembled into a train of up to fifty cars and then rushed to the mill by a plantation locomotive for processing of the cane, within a 72-hour window after which the sugar content of the cane would drop dramatically. Then, after the cane had been removed from a given field, the portable track would be broken down and hauled back to the "main line," then hauled to the next set of fields that were ready for harvest, where the portable track would again be laid.

In the late 1930's and early 1940's, plantations began investigating the use of alternative hauling equipment that had the potential of improving harvesting productivity. Although delayed by WWII, the plantations after the War began to replace their fleets of small railway cane cars, locomotives and portable track with large tractor-trailers or newly developed 30 or 40-ton specialized cane hauling "Tournahaulers" that could go into fields where cane was being cut and then carry the cane directly to the mill, thereby eliminating the need for their agricultural railroads. As trucks and their diesel engines became larger and more reliable, it became only a matter of time until all of the plantations railways would be gone.

Wartime photography restrictions on Oahu reduced the opportunities for documenting these interesting plantation railways. Victor Norton apparently waited until after the end of the War to venture out to the sugar mills where the various enginehouses were located. During 1945 and 1946, Victor Norton visited five of Oahu's sugar plantations to photograph their railway equipment. Of the sugar plantations with operating railways, he visited the Oahu Sugar Company in Waipahu, the Ewa Plantation Company, the Waianae Plantation Company and the Waialua Agricultural Company. Sometimes he was lucky and found equipment working, while other times cane was not being harvested and so operations were not in progress. When it was not possible to film operations, he made static roster shots of equipment at rest. When Victor finally visited Waimanalo Plantation, which had abandoned its rail operations in 1944, he found two of their locomotives truly buried in the weeds, but, being a true railfan, he photographed them anyway. Victor's coverage of Oahu Sugar Company and Ewa Plantation Company equipment was quite complete. On the other hand, he never visited Honolulu Plantation in Aiea (even though when first stationed at Pearl Harbor, he lived in a "tent city" right along their main line) nor Kahuku Plantation on Oahu's northern tip. And, his trips to Waianae and Waialua appeared to have been quite brief.

Bill Blewett, on the other hand, being a security person, obviously felt more comfortable photographing items such as ancient plantation locomotives that clearly had no strategic value. Although Bill was reassigned to the Mainland on July 1, 1945, just before the War in the Pacific ended, he had by then visited all seven of Oahu's plantations -- getting around by hitching rides on military vehicles that seemed to be going everywhere on Oahu -- and photographed their equipment on 116 size film. Like Victor, he too had almost complete coverage of Oahu Sugar and Ewa Plantation equipment, but also Waianae -- probably because of these three lines' proximity to his base. However, his coverage of the other plantations was also incomplete.

As mentioned previously, Grant Oakes, Jr., photographed much of the equipment at Waialua, which rounded out that plantation, and Bob Zinsmeister contributed two scenes each of Ewa Plantation and Oahu Sugar, but it was Victor's trading/buying photos after the War, which gave us access to the scenes taken by Vitaly Uzoff and Kent Cochrane, which really complete the Oahu scene.

This chapter then documents these servicemen's visits to Oahu's lesser known railways. Our understanding of railway operations in Hawaii during this period of time has certainly been enhanced due to their efforts. Our hats go off to all of them!

Honolulu Plantation Co., Aiea -- 36" Gauge

ABOVE: This is one of the few photographs of a Honolulu Plantation locomotive under steam. *Puuloa*, HPC #4, was an 0-6-2T plantation locomotive built in 1901 by the Baldwin Locomotive Works in their Philadelphia plant. This little locomotive lived a charmed life -- after some 46 years on the Honolulu Plantation, it was sold first to Oahu Sugar Co. as their #7, and then in 1965 to the Camino, Cable and Northern Railroad in Camino, California. *Puuloa* is now back in Hawaii and is on display at the Plantation Village museum in Waipahu. Photo by Bill Blewett.

Honolulu Plantation was located north and east of Pearl Harbor. The first plantation on this land started in the 1850's, and like Hawaii's other plantations at that time, there was no railway, so cane was hauled to the mill on large wagons pulled by teams of oxen. When the sugar mill burned in the 1870's the plantation became ranchland until the 1890's when the land again became a sugar plantation. After a reorganization in 1900 that plantation became the Honolulu Plantation Company that lasted through WWII. Jesse Conde's research for *Sugar Trains* found the first mention of their railway in a 1901 report that indicated that the plantation had just purchased 400 more cane cars to give them a total of 500. Over the next forty years the plantation expanded inland as Honolulu Plantation lost more and more of its land near Pearl Harbor to the U.S. Government for portions of present day Pearl Harbor Naval Station, John Rodgers Airfield (today's Honolulu International Airport) and

Hickam Air Base. In 1931 the plantation railway system consisted of five steam locomotives and 500 five-ton cane cars (some equipped with roller bearings!) operating on 36.5 miles of permanent and six miles of portable track. "Fluming" (floating cane in narrow channels of water from a higher elevations to a rail transfer station) was used to bring cane stalks down to the railway from some of the plantation's upper fields.

Additional Honolulu Plantation lands were taken by the U.S. Government in both 1940 and 1944, and one locomotive that became excess, #2, *Waimalu*, was sold to the Kahuku Plantation in 1944. The plantation railway main line was replaced by trucks in mid-1945, and the company sold its remaining fields and much of its railway equipment, including 0-6-2T #4, *Puuloa*, to neighboring Oahu Sugar Co. on the first of January 1947. In 1948, two additional 0-6-2T's, #1 and #5 (*Halawa* and *Manana*) were sold to the Hawaiian Philippine Sugar Company, with its mill on the island

No.	Name	Type	Builder & No.	Year	Notes
1	*Halawa*	0-6-2T + Tender	Baldwin #16438	Jan 1899	To Hawaiian-Philippine Sugar Co., 1948; Currently being restored in California.
3	*Aiea*	0-6-2T	Baldwin #16333	Oct 1898	From American Sugar Co., Molokai, 1901.
4	*Puuloa*	0-6-2T + Tender	Baldwin #19741	Nov 1901	To Oahu Sugar Co., 1947.
5	*Manana*	0-6-2T	Baldwin #43246	Apr 1916	To Hawaiian-Philippine Sugar Co., 1948; Currently being restored in California.

Honolulu Plantation Co., Aiea -- 36" Gauge Locomotive Roster in 1945:

ABOVE: Victor Norton did not start photographing Oahu's cane railways until after the War, so he missed photographing these locomotives himself. He purchased these two photographs after he returned home. Here is Honolulu Plantation #1, *Halawa*, an 0-6-2T that was actually Honolulu Plantation's second locomotive, posed outside their Aiea enginehouse without her four-wheeled tender. The little locomotive survived over fifty years at a sugar plantation in the Philippines and is now being rebuilt in California. Photographer unknown, but probably Vitaly Uzoff. Collection of Victor Norton, Jr.

BELOW: Here is another view of *Puuloa*, 0-6-2T #4. The date on the back of this photo is May 1945, right before Honolulu Plantation eliminated the main lines of its railway system. She was the largest of HPC's locomotives, with 33-inch driving wheels and 12x16-inch cylinders. Note that *Puuloa's* four-wheeled tender has also been removed. As an interesting side note, the OR&L timesheet from September 24, 1942, showed that "Hon Plant #4" made two round-trip runs from OR&L's Halawa interchange with the Navy at Pearl Harbor to their Oahu Sugar interchange at Waipahu Mill, possibly with train-loads of ammunition headed to the Navy's magazines on former Oahu Sugar Company property. Photographer unknown, but probably Vitaly Uzoff. Collection of Victor Norton, Jr.

of Negros in the Philippines. Both locomotives operated there into the 1990's, and they were both recently purchased by a newly incorporated organization called the Kauai Plantation Railway. They are now at Brook's Locomotive Works in Georgetown, California, where they are currently being rebuilt. If all goes well, the pair may soon be running in tourist service on the island of Kauai.

It should be noted that Honolulu Plantation was the only sugar company in Hawaii that actually refined sugar here in the islands, primarily for the local pineapple canneries. All the others simply ground the sugar in their mills and then sent the partially processed "raw sugar" to Mainland United States for refining.

Even though Honolulu Plantation sat adjacent to Pearl Harbor, and therefore should have been the most accessible of Oahu's plantations, wartime photography restrictions and the early elimination of their railway system meant that very few photographs of HPC equipment were taken by our servicemen railfans.

ABOVE: The crew of Oahu Sugar Co. #6, a Baldwin 0-6-2T named *Koalipea*, receives instructions from the supervisor in the broad-brimmed hat before returning to work. Photo by Victor Norton, Jr., Hawaiian Railway Society Collection.

In *Sugar Trains*, Jesse Conde provided documentation showing that a plantation railway was an integral part of the Oahu Sugar Company from its inception by Benjamin F. Dillingham in 1894. The original plantation covered twenty square miles of leased lands in the vicinity of Waipahu, including Ford's Island in the center of Pearl Harbor, from which cane was brought to the mainland of Oahu via ferry boat. Unfortunately, there is no indication in any of the records discovered to date as to whether the ferry carried the cane from the island in bundles on deck, on animal-drawn wagons or on cane cars that rode across Pearl Harbor on rails installed on the deck of the ferry. That unique operation lasted only until 1917 when the U.S. Navy requisitioned the island to build an airfield on what we now know as Ford Island.

OSC's original plantation was irrigated by artesian wells, so its growth was somewhat limited until an Oahu Sugar subsidiary, the Waihole Water Company (using two Shays and one electric storage battery mining locomotive) punched a tunnel through the Koolau Mountain range in 1916 to bring 125-150 million gallons of water per day from Oahu's Windward Coast. Oahu Sugar's plantation railway grew significantly after that and by 1939 consisted of sixty miles of permanent three-foot gauge track plus an unspecified amount of portable track. Over this track operated a total of 939 plantation cars, including 860 four-ton cane cars, fifty cars for carrying portable track and twenty-nine other cars. Water flumes were also used to bring cane from the higher elevations of the plantation. Over the years the plantation owned a total of ten

No.	Name	Type	Builder & No.	Year	Notes
1	*Waipahu*	0-6-2T	Baldwin #15321	May 1897	To Dale Gentry, San Bernardino, CA, 1954
3	*Waikele*	0-6-2T	Baldwin #17911	Jul 1900	
4	*Waiawa*	0-6-2T	Baldwin #18022	Aug 1900	
5	*Waikakalaua*	0-6-2T	Baldwin #32816	Jun 1908	To Travel Town, Los Angeles, 1954
6	*Koalipea*	0-6-2T	Baldwin #44661	Jan 1917	
8	*Hoaeae*	0-6-0	Porter #6922	Jul 1924	
9	*Waikane*	0-4-0T + Tender	Porter #4030	Jan 1908	From U.S. Army Corps of Engineers, year unknown.

Oahu Sugar Co., Waipahu -- 36" Gauge Locomotive Roster in 1945:

ABOVE: This photograph was used in Volume 2 to show the difference in construction standards between the OR&L on the right and a plantation railway, Oahu Sugar Co., on the left. It is repeated here for the same reason. Differences include lighter rail, little or no ballast and simpler turnouts for the plantation railway. The location is Waikakalaua Canyon, inland and north of the protected diamond where the two lines crossed. As described in the previous volume, this is believed to be the location where OSC's main line north from the mill split to climb to the cane fields on the plateaus on either side of the canyon, and the chimney is one of the pumping stations to provide water for irrigation from Oahu's aquifer. Photo by Victor Norton, Jr., Hawaiian Railway Society Collection.

steam locomotives, including one transferred from the Honolulu Plantation Company when Oahu Sugar absorbed that plantation in 1947. During World War II Oahu Sugar cooperated closely with the government, and *Sugar Trains* includes a photograph of an ammunition train at a military check point, with gates manned by sentries, on one of Oahu Sugar's railway lines. One other picture of particular interest in *Sugar Trains* shows Oahu Sugar's thirty-ton capacity cane

cars operating in 1947. These were the largest cane cars in Hawaii, and they truly dwarfed their plantation locomotives. Oahu Sugar started using large cane trucks in 1946 -- at first only to haul cane from their fields to rail transfer points -- and they eliminated their railway system in late 1950. Oahu Sugar Company's processed sugar was carried from the Waipahu mill to Honolulu by the OR&L until that railroad abandoned its main line at the end of 1947.

BELOW: The next several views show Victor's introduction to Oahu Sugar Company's rail facilities near their Waipahu mill. The first thing he encountered was a trainload of sugar cane stalks. Under the jumble of cane stalks are four-wheeled, chain side four-ton capacity cane cars. In previous decades the cars would have been loaded by the "Hapa Ko" method, with bundles of uniform cane stalks carried up a wooden plank and stacked neatly in the car. However, once mobile cranes were reliable enough to be used in the fields, the labor-intensive Hapa Ko system was eliminated and "grabs" of cane stalks were lifted from piles and dropped onto the little cars as shown. Photo by Victor Norton, Jr., Hawaiian Railway Society Collection.

OPPOSITE ABOVE: Further down the track Victor received his first view of OSC's enginehouse and their huge sugar mill in the background, still with camouflaged smokestacks. In the scene from left to right are two OSC work cars, locomotive #6, plus the line-up of #4, #1 and #9. OR&L boxcar #430, which will be moved to the mill for a load of bagged sugar, is on the right. Both photos opposite page by Victor Norton, Jr., Hawaiian Railway Society Collection.

OPPOSITE BELOW: Here is a view of the same scene from another angle, fortunately in bright sun. Again we see OSC 0-6-2T numbers 4 and 1, and 0-4-0T number 9 with her four-wheeled tender.

TOP: OSC #1, *Waipahu*, was Oahu Sugar Company's first locomotive. Originally built as a coal-burner, she and her sisters (and the mill boilers) were converted to burn oil in 1907. Note that #1 has two builders plates -- this was common practice on Oahu for locomotives that had received replacement boilers. Photo by Victor Norton, Jr., Hawaiian Railway Society Collection.

ABOVE: Another view of Oahu Sugar #1, this time showing the right side of the locomotive. In the background is Shell tank car #505, which presumably is carrying a load of heavy fuel oil from Honolulu Harbor via the OR&L for OSC's little locomotives or their sugar mill boilers. Photo by Bill Blewett.

BELOW: One of five Baldwin 0-6-2T's that Oahu Sugar owned over the years, this is #3, *Waikele*. She was built with 33-inch drivers and 12x16-inch cylinders. Photo by Victor Norton, Jr., Hawaiian Railway Society Collection.

BOTTOM: Bill Blewett caught #3 under steam, with a four-wheeled flatcar carrying one of the big "cane grabs" used by OSC's mobile cranes to load sugar cane stalks in their fields. Photo by Bill Blewett.

Here are two views of #5, *Waiakalaua*, yet another thirty-ton 0-6-2T plantation locomotive from Baldwin. This locomotive survives today in Travel Town in Los Angeles' Griffith Park, having been moved there in 1954. Both photos by Bill Blewett.

OPPOSITE: One of the problems that railfan photographers have faced over the years are poles between their subject and them. The OSC enginehouse had a line of poles on the south (normally sunny) side for fuel, water and lights. It is interesting to see in these two views of #4, *Waiawa*, how each of our photographers decided to handle this problem. As shown above, Victor Norton chose to take the wide shot and ignore the pole, while Bill Blewett took a tight, front-3/4 view as shown below.

TOP: Looking at the basic wooden engine shed in the background, I am continuously amazed that Oahu Sugar was able to make its locomotives sparkle like #6 above. Even more amazing was their ability to not only keep their little fleet running, but to modernize their locomotives (note the steam generator for the electric headlight behind the bell) and do heavy repairs like boiler replacements (note the second builders plate). Victor Norton, Jr., Hawaiian Ry. Society.

ABOVE: Number 6, *Koalipea*, was the most modern of OSC's 0-6-2T locomotives. She was built by Baldwin Locomotive Works of Philadelphia in January of 1917, the last of four nearly identical 0-6-2T's. The little thirty-tonner looks almost as good as she must have when she left the plant nearly three decades before. Photo by Bill Blewett.

BELOW: This is Oahu Sugar's last new locomotive, 0-6-0 #8, *Hoaeae*, built by H.K. Porter in 1924. *Hoaeae* was also their largest locomotive, weighing in at 38 tons. She had 36-inch wheels and 13x18-inch cylinders. Bill Blewett photo.

BOTTOM: Victor did the best he could with the poles on the sunny side of the servicing area. In spite of that distraction, a lot can still be learned about *Hoaeae* from this photograph. In addition to the specific details, notice the relative size of #8 when compared to #1, just behind #8's tender. Victor Norton, Jr., Hawaiian Ry. Society Collection.

BELOW: 0-6-0 switchers with slope-back tenders (for better visibility when backing) were relatively rare on American narrow gauge railways, so it's nice to have this rear 3/4 view to see its details. The forward (taller) bunker held heavy oil for the boiler, while the balance of the tank held water for making steam. Photo by Victor Norton, Jr., Hawaiian Railway Society Collection.

BOTTOM: Bill Blewett caught this rear view of *Hoaeae* working a string of empty cane cars in the yard near Oahu Sugar's mill in Waipahu. Photo by Bill Blewett.

TOP: *Waikane*, #9, was an 0-4-0T with a four-wheeled tender. It was built by H.K. Porter for the U.S. Army Corps of Engineers in 1908, and came to Oahu Sugar from Seattle, although the year of its purchase is unknown. Of interest is #9's "blackout" headlight, still in place after the end of the War. Victor Norton, Jr., Hawaiian Ry. Society Collection.

ABOVE: With her bell ringing wildly for the crossing, *Waikane* crosses one of the company roads near the Waipahu mill with a string of Fricke four-ton capacity chain side cane cars. Photo by Bill Blewett.

BELOW: Bob Zinsmeister also made a trip to Waipahu to photograph Oahu Sugar's locomotives, and managed to find a few of them during his short visit. Shown first is #3, *Waikele*, with her engineer posing in the cab doorway. Note tank car #1401 on the siding above #3, presumably filling the fuel tank to the right of the locomotive.

BOTTOM: 0-4-0T #9, *Waikane*, sits outside the enginehouse in almost the same position that Victor had found her. Even small steam locomotives like these required a lot of maintenance. Note the hose under the cab, perhaps for filling or draining her boiler? Both photos this page by Bob Zinsmeister.

TOP: According to *Sugar Trains*, Oahu Sugar built a new shop building in 1921, "with facilities to overhaul locomotives and steam plows." Here we see one of OSC's Baldwins, quite possibly #5, in the shop for boiler work. Look closely at the bottom of the missing board on the left front facade, and you will find the shop's boiler flue storage. Photo by Victor Norton, Jr., Hawaiian Railway Society Collection.

ABOVE: Here is Bill Blewett's going away shot of #9 and her little tender. Since none of OSC's other tank engines had tenders, this one presumably came with the little 0-4-0T when it was purchased from the Army. Photo by Bill Blewett.

These are two views of Oahu Sugar Company non-revenue equipment. The cars shown below are double-trucked Gregg flatcars, used to haul the hundreds of workers that were needed to produce sugar cane to and from the fields. On a typical day these workers might burn a field ready for harvesting to remove leaves from the stalks, or cut the stalks and prepare them for loading into cane cars, while others prepared the temporary rights-of-way for the portable tracks that went out into these fields. In recently harvested fields, laborers plowed the fields and then planted pieces of stalks for the next crop and then continuously irrigated or fertilized them. Almost all of Oahu Sugar's plantation workers lived in villages of company-owned houses near the mill, and commuted to and from their workplaces on these passenger cars. On the opposite page is a four-wheeled tank car that was built on the frame of a sugar cane car. Both photos by Victor Norton, Jr., Hawaiian Railway Society Collection.

OPPOSITE BELOW: *Waikele* sits patiently while waiting for Oahu Railway tank car #952 to be filled with molasses, a by-product of sugar refining, from the big tank behind the locomotive. Molasses would usually be shipped to Honolulu for transfer to a waiting ship, but if a surplus could not be sold, it would be taken to a growing field and recycled as fertilizer. Photo by Bill Blewett.

ABOVE: *Ewa*, Ewa Plantation's first locomotive, was built for the sugar company by Baldwin in 1890. She is shown here during the War years with a blackout cover on her headlight which would allow a little light to shine on the track ahead for night operations without becoming a target for any enemy submarines lurking off the coast of Oahu. This beautiful portrait was taken by the U.S. Marine Corps' Bill Blewett, who was stationed at the nearby Ewa Marine Corps Air Station until shortly before the War's end.

Until 1879, when James Campbell brought to Oahu the technology to drill artesian wells to tap subterranean aquifers of fresh water, his vast landholdings on the broad, flat and very dry Ewa Coral Plain could be used for little more than cattle ranching. However, once a plentiful supply of fresh water was assured, that "wasteland" became prime sugar country. Ewa Plantation was the brainchild of Benjamin F. Dillingham, who envisioned a sugar plantation on land leased from Mr. Campbell as a primary source of traffic for his fledgling Oahu Railway. His plantation had the potential to cover some 10,000 acres of relatively flat land, so a railway system was considered essential from the plantation's inception. Per *Sugar Trains*, work on the three-foot gauge Ewa Plantation railway began on January 6, 1890, and it was operating with a rented OR&L locomotive that September. Ewa's first locomotive arrived in early October. Unlike so many of the other plantations where little or no information was available, Jesse Conde found a wealth of information on the history of Ewa Plantation and its railway, and *Sugar Trains* contains several highly detailed newspaper and plantation generated articles about railway operations there, including the laying of portable track, manually loading cane and using animals (mules, donkeys and horses) to haul the loaded cane cars along the portable track to the main line of the plantation railway.

No.	Name	Type	Builder & No.	Year	Notes
		Ewa Plantation Co., Ewa -- 36" Gauge Locomotive Roster in 1945:			
1	*Ewa*	0-4-2T + Tender	Baldwin #10755	Mar 1890	On display, Hawaiian Railway Society, Ewa
3	*Waimanalo*	0-6-0T + Tender	Baldwin #14991	Aug 1896	
4	*Sampson*	0-6-2T + Tender	Baldwin #17442	Feb 1900	Ordered for American Sugar Co., Molokai
5	*Nanakuli*	0-6-0T + Tender	Baldwin #17655	Apr 1900	
6	*E. P. Co.*	0-6-2T + Tender	Baldwin #25710	May 1905	
7	*Geo. F. Renton, Jr.*	2-6-2	Baldwin #57851	Jul 1924	
8	---	B	Plymouth	?	
9	---	B	Plymouth	?	

BELOW: Here is a scene that could have come from almost any American shortline in the 1940's. The large steel water tank and Armstrong turntable were, however, quite unusual for a Hawaiian plantation, and the well-manicured lawn shows the pride that Ewa Plantation's management and employees had in their railway system. Photo by Victor Norton, Jr., Hawaiian Railway Society Collection.

BELOW: Victor Norton had nothing but good things to say about Ewa Plantation's railway, but he was particularly impressed with their roundhouse, remembering that, "It was so clean, you could have eaten off the floor!" The roundhouse was built in 1924 with a concrete facade that looked more modern than the remainder of the corrugated iron building, and it remained intact until the 1970's. If you look closely, you can see the frame of 2-6-2 #7 in the left stall and the nose of diesel #8 or #9 in the rightmost one. Photo by Victor Norton, Jr., Hawaiian Railway Society Collection.

To cover such a large area, Ewa Plantation in 1931 owned almost 29 miles of permanent track, eight miles of portable track (in fifteen-foot sections weighing 90 to 100 pounds each), seven steam locomotives, 627 cane cars and 78 other cars used for different tasks such as carrying workers to the fields and transporting bagged sugar, molasses, fertilizer and portable track sections. (This data, listed in *Sugar Trains*, originally came from Gilmore's *Hawaiian Sugar Manual*.)

Ewa Plantation ordered its last locomotives, two small mechanical single-truckers from Plymouth, in 1941 to replace one of their ailing steam locomotives that needed an unavailable replacement boiler. Experimentation with large diesel cane transporters called "Tournahaulers" began in 1946, and Ewa quickly phased out its railroad before the end of the 1947 sugar season. Ewa Plantation's bagged sugar was transported to the port of Honolulu by the Oahu Railway and Land Company until that line was abandoned at the end of 1947.

We are fortunate that both Bill Blewett and Victor Norton spent several photography sessions at Ewa Plantation. Although the little plantation steam locomotives were their principal quarry, they also did a fine job of documenting the railway's roundhouse and turntable, plus numerous background structures. Between them they photographed all but three of the line's locomotives, both having missed *Geo. F. Renton, Jr.*, #7, a 2-6-2 built by Baldwin Locomotive Works in 1924, and Plymouth diesels #8 and #9. The former sat out the War years in pieces in the roundhouse, while the latter were just little internal combustion industrial locos that would not have been "film worthy" to a die-hard steam fan.

OPPOSITE AND ABOVE: Here are two views by Bill Blewett showing Ewa's Roundhouse and turntable. Cane harvesting must have been in full swing, since all of the stalls are empty in his roundhouse photograph. His view of the plantation's turntable above shows locomotive #1, *Ewa*, between assignments. Both photos by Bill Blewett.

OPPOSITE ABOVE: In this view, we see what a simple little engine #1 was. Since plantation locomotives and cane cars had only handbrakes, there was no need for an air compressor. She did, however, have an electrical generator for her headlight, and a hand-operated whistle and bell -- both of which were obviously kept very well polished.

OPPOSITE BELOW: In addition to hauling cane cars to and from the fields, little *Ewa #1* did its share of switching around the mill. Here the diminutive 0-4-2T backs with an OR&L outside braced boxcar that will soon be loaded with bags of raw sugar for shipment from Honolulu Harbor. Both photos opposite page by Bill Blewett.

ABOVE: Victor Norton visited Ewa on a very slow day and found #1 resting peacefully in her roundhouse stall. The sturdy 0-4-2T, built by Baldwin in 1890, resides today as a display at the Hawaiian Railway Museum in Ewa, quite close to where she labored for over fifty years. If you look to the right of #1, you will see a partial view of Plymouth #9. Photo by Victor Norton, Jr., Hawaiian Railway Society Collection.

ABOVE: These are Bob Zinsmeister's two Ewa Plantation photos. On his one trip to Ewa he found 0-4-2T #1 sitting outside of the roundhouse. This view of the roundhouse shows that although the front of the building had a modern concrete facade, the rest was constructed of steel panels. Bob's other Ewa photograph shows 0-6-0 #3 switching an OR&L car. Tank cars like #952 were usually used for transporting molasses, a by-product of the sugar manufacturing process. Both photos this page by Bob Zinsmeister.

OPPOSITE: Victor Norton also snapped a few views of one of Ewa's little plantation locomotives switching much larger OR&L boxcars. Here again is 0-6-0T #3, *Waimanalo*, with two outside braced wood and steel boxcars. Both photos on opposite page by Victor Norton, Jr., Hawaiian Railway Society Collection.

BELOW: Bill Blewett caught up with 0-6-0T #3 in the main cane yard pulling two plantation non-revenue cars, the second of which is obviously much wider than the first, while the unknown locomotive on the right waits for access to the main line through the yard. Photo by Bill Blewett.

OPPOSITE: Bill Blewett snapped these two views of #5, *Nanakuli*, an 0-6-0T from 1900 with a company-added four-wheeled tender, spotting an OR&L boxcar for loading bags of raw sugar. OR&L's boxcars typically had round roofs covered with corrugated steel, and more often than not ladder rungs beside the door on each side to provide access to the roof. In the top scene, #5 pushes a boxcar backwards from Ewa's "main line" and then spots it at the "high security" loading area in the lower photo. Note #5's coupler, designed so that it can handle standard knuckle couplers on interchange equipment, as well as links on plantation cars. Both photos by Bill Blewett.

BELOW: Visiting during the quiet season, Victor found several of Ewa's locomotives slumbering in their assigned stalls. This is #4, *Samson*, an 0-6-2T originally purchased from Baldwin by the American Sugar Company on the neighboring island of Molokai. When American Sugar failed in 1900, *Samson* was quickly diverted to Oahu and then assigned to Ewa Plantation. Photo by Victor Norton, Jr., Hawaiian Railway Society Collection.

OPPOSITE ABOVE: 0-6-2T #4 works the main cane yard in Ewa. When cane was being harvested, as many locomotives as possible were in operation. The cane stalks needed to get into the mill for processing within 72 hours of being cut in order to prevent a rapid deterioration of sugar quality. Photo by Bill Blewett.

OPPOSITE BELOW: Since Victor's only shot of #5 was inside the plantation roundhouse, he purchased this nice view of the little 0-6-0T after the War. Unfortunately, the identification of the photographer is not known. Collection of Victor Norton, Jr.

Hello Jim,
This is payback time for all the R.R. mags. you've sent me - This mag. (album) has some of my Oahu photos in it.
Bill

LEFT: Most of Ewa Plantation's railway cars were three or four-ton capacity cane cars that had been built in the company's shop from purchased "kits." These kits consisted of little more than the metal components -- the customer was required to provide the wooden parts from local sources. These little four-wheeled platforms were quite adaptable for other purposes. Here we see two of Ewa's home-made boxcars flanking one of their flat cars. Photo by Victor Norton, Jr., Hawaiian Railway Society Collection.

ABOVE: Ewa Plantation #6 was an 0-6-2T built by Baldwin in 1905. She is shown out in one of Ewa's cane fields in front of an empty flare side door cane car that had derailed. Photo by Bill Blewett.

OPPOSITE ABOVE: Ewa Plantation operated its railway in a manner quite comparable to a Mainland U.S. railroad. The line had a formal rulebook, and as you can see in this scene, it had automated wig-wag crossing signals and even semaphores. These controlled the entrance to this stretch of two-way single track just east of the mill, where the lines from the southern (on the right) and eastern fields joined just before crossing Renton Road -- the principal road into the company town of Ewa. Photo by Victor Norton, Jr., Hawaiian Railway Society Collection.

OPPOSITE BELOW: This appears to be the south end of the cane unloading yard for the Ewa Mill. Victor captured this scene during the two-month period when cane was not being harvested; otherwise, the tracks on the left would have been filled with loaded cars waiting their turn to enter the unloading area dead ahead. Photo by Victor Norton, Jr., Hawaiian Railway Society Collection.

Hawaiian Railway Album

ABOVE: Waianae Sugar Company's enginehouse is a narrow gauge modeler's delight. Shown here are all three of WSC's locomotives: Number 1, *H.A. Widemann*, in the left stall of the enginehouse; Number 2, *Waianae*, outside, behind Fricke chain side cane car #62; and, if you look very closely at the very back of the right stall, you can see the bell and tank of *Kaala*, a Fowler 0-4-2T built in 1883! (Unfortunately no one went around back to photograph *Kaala*....) Photo by Victor Norton, Jr., Hawaiian Railway Society Collection.

Waianae Sugar Company had one of the earliest plantation railways in the Kingdom. According to Jesse Conde in his *Fowler Locomotives in the Kingdom of Hawaii*, a steam locomotive was purchased from England's Ransome and Rapier in 1879, and it arrived at Waianae before the end of that year. Track for their thirty-inch gauge Fowler plantation railway was installed in February of 1880. The railway was quite successful, and within two years a second small steam locomotive was ordered, this time from the Fowler Company. Hawaii's King Kalakaua, an enthusiastic fan of new technology, twice during 1884 visited the plantation and rode the new trains on Waianae Sugar's seven and one-half miles of track, through their cane fields in the Makaha, Waianae and Lualualei valleys.

Until the Oahu Railway worked its way up the Leeward Coast in 1895, raw sugar was shipped to Honolulu via ship from the plantation's wharf at Waianae. According to *Sugar Trains*, again quoting from Gilmore's *Hawaii Sugar Manual*, the Waianae

Plantation's railway by 1931 had supplanted all of their water flumes and consisted of the following: 14.2 miles of thirty-inch permanent track, 2.84 miles of portable track, three steam locomotives including the Fowler from 1883, 140 three-ton cane cars and 54 miscellaneous plantation work cars. In *Sugar Trains*, Jesse Conde reported that he had found a 1940 account that also described a "wise old white horse" that switched the cane cars in the mill yard at that time.

High labor costs forced the plantation out of business in 1947, and the plantation railway and mill equipment were sold, presumably all for scrap -- but not before several servicemen/railfans had discovered it and recorded the following images on film for us.

Waianae Sugar Co., Waianae -- 30" Gauge Locomotive Roster in 1945:					
No.	Name	Type	Builder & No.	Year	Notes
--	*Kaala*	0-4-2T + Tender	Fowler #5574	1883	
1	*H.A. Widemann*	0-6-0T + Tender	Baldwin #16925	Jul 1899	
2	*Waianae*	0-4-2T + Tender	Baldwin #23449	Dec 1903	

ABOVE: One of Victor Norton's Navy buddies, Bob Marquet, hams it up for the camera in the cab of Waianae Sugar Co. #2. Compared to the large locomotives on the Mainland, this tiny 30-inch gauge, seven-ton 0-4-0T must have looked to have been little more than a toy. Photo by Victor Norton, Jr., Hawaiian Railway Society Collection.

OPPOSITE ABOVE: Bill Blewett caught up with *H.A. Widemann* as she was taking on water. This little 0-6-0T was built by Baldwin in 1899 and, weighing in at eleven tons, was Waianae Sugar's largest locomotive. The sand bags on the pilot were for extra traction. They provided weight for the front end when unopened, but when that was not enough, the bags would be opened and the sand sprinkled on the rails by hand. Photo by Bill Blewett.

OPPOSITE BELOW: Here is a nice left side view of *H.A. Widemann*. She really was a basic side-tank locomotive, although she did at least have a steam generator for her headlight. *H. A. Widemann* was built with 30-inch wheels and 9x14-inch cylinders. Photo by Bill Blewett.

ABOVE: *Waianae*, a saddle-tank 0-4-2T locomotive, was four years younger than *H.A. Widemann*, but had two less drivers and weighed only seven tons. Her drivers were 26 inches in diameter and her cylinders measured only seven inches in diameter with a twelve-inch stroke. All three of Waianae Sugar's locomotives had homebuilt four-wheeled tenders to extend their range between water stops. Photo by Bill Blewett.

ABOVE: This view of the Waianae mill, looking south in late 1945 or early 1946, shows their smokestack still in camouflage paint. Waianae was on the western edge of Oahu, and no one wanted the mill to be a target for enemy ships or submarines lying off the Leeward Coast. Photo by Victor Norton, Jr., Hawaiian Railway Society Collection.

BELOW: Here is another view of the mill, this time looking north. The mechanical cane unloader is in the lean-to in the center. Note the light thirty-inch gauge track and the three-way stub switch in the foreground. Photo by Victor Norton, Jr., Hawaiian Railway Society Collection.

BELOW: The Coast Guard's Kent Cochrane also visited Waianae Sugar Co. before the plantation closed, and he snapped this view of #1, *H.A. Widemann*, near the line's small wooden water tank. It's too bad that he did not get more of the interesting little four-wheeled tender just to the right of the locomotive's cab. Photo by Kent W. Cochrane, Collection of Victor Norton, Jr.

OPPOSITE ABOVE: This beautiful photograph, another one by Kent Cochrane of New Britain, Connecticut, was purchased by Victor to fill out his Oahu railroad album. It shows the left side of #2 and Waianae Sugar's deteriorating enginehouse, both in perfect light conditions. Photo by Kent W. Cochrane, Collection of Victor Norton, Jr.

OPPOSITE BELOW: Victor purchased this photograph from the Army's Vitaly Uzoff. The date on the reverse is given as "3-20-46" and it shows not a "wise old white horse," but rather just a common mule, switching a three-ton cane car at Waianae's mill. This must have been the last use of animal power by any of Hawaii's plantation railways. Photo by Vitaly V. Uzoff, Collection of Victor Norton, Jr.

ABOVE: Waiting patiently during the off-season is Waialua Agricultural Company's second #2, a 28-ton 2-6-0 with forty-inch drivers, that had been purchased from Kahului Railroad on Maui in September of 1937. Photo by Victor Norton, Jr., Hawaiian Railway Society Collection.

Early records uncovered by Jesse Conde indicate that sugar cane was grown in the Waialua area as early as 1836 by one of Oahu's first missionaries. However, it was not until 1898, when Benjamin F. Dillingham and his associates purchased the surrounding property, reorganized it as the Waialua Agricultural Company and brought much needed investment to it, that a plantation there became a success. As could have been expected, construction of a plantation railway began in 1899, shortly after Mr. Dillingham became involved with the property, and that railway was continuously expanded and upgraded as the plantation grew inland to higher elevations, further from the coast. By 1931 the railway reached its maximum size as the plantation replaced all of its water flumes except those from the highest, most inaccessible fields. At that time, according to Gilmore's *Hawaii Sugar Manual*, as quoted in *Sugar Trains*, the Waialua Agricultural railway system consisted of six steam locomotives, 685 cane cars, 23 mud-press cars (for carrying sugar residue back to the fields to be used as fertilizer), 25 miscellaneous work cars, 55 miles of permanent track and eight miles of portable track. In 1937 the plantation purchased two additional steam locomotives from Maui's Kahului Railroad, and sometime later purchased two small Plymouth diesel-mechanical

Waialua Agricultural Co., Waialua -- 36" Gauge Locomotive Roster in 1945:

No.	Name	Type	Builder & No.	Year	Notes
1		0-6-0T	Baldwin #16453	Jan 1899	
2		2-6-0	Baldwin #23763	Feb 1904	Formerly Kahului Railroad #5
3		0-6-2T	Baldwin #17385	Jan 1900	No WWII photos of #3 were found, so it may have been gone by 1945
4		0-6-2T	Baldwin #18700	Feb 1901	
5		0-6-2T	Baldwin #18701	Feb 1901	
6		0-6-2T	Waialua Ag. Co.	1919	Built in co. shop from spare parts Now at Hawaiian Railway Museum
7		2-6-2	Baldwin #31125	Jun 1907	Formerly Kahului Railroad #8
8		B	Plymouth	?	Diesel-mechanical yard switcher
9		B	Plymouth	?	Diesel-mechanical yard switcher

ABOVE: Victor Norton visited Waialua during the few months when sugar cane was not being harvested. Although he found no equipment in operation, he did take this excellent photograph of Waialua Agricultural Company's engine-house/shop on the left and sugar mill on the right beyond the cane cars. Photo by Victor Norton, Jr., Hawaiian Railway Society Collection.

locomotives for yard switching service. The track gauge was three feet, just like OR&L's, and Waialua's raw sugar was shipped from their mill to Honolulu on the Oahu Railway.

Very shortly after the attack on Pearl Harbor, the U.S. Army extended Waialua Agricultural's railway up Helemano Ridge and built a connection with the OR&L's pineapple branch at Brodie Junction, north of the town of Wahiawa. Although never used by the OR&L, it remained throughout the war as a contingency to service Oahu's North Shore, just in case OR&L's main line around Keana Point were to be cut by another enemy attack.

Unlike many of Hawaii's other plantations, Waialua Agricultural was not anxious to replace their railway system with trucks. According to *Sugar Trains*, this conversion was first influenced by OR&L's abandonment of their main line from Kahuku to Honolulu at the end of 1947, after which the plantation had no choice but to join a railroad subsidiary and two other plantations, Ewa Plantation and Oahu Sugar, in forming a new company to truck raw sugar from Waialua and the other mills to Honolulu Harbor. Even after that Waialua Agricultural's conversion from a railway system to thirty-ton Tournahauler cane haulers was not completed until 1952.

BELOW: Bill Blewett also visited during one of the mill's slow months and found Baldwin 0-6-2T #5 sitting cold behind the enginehouse. The car in front of #5 is a sand car, normally run in front of a locomotive as shown here. One or two men would sit in the car and, when slippery rails were encountered, would pour sand down the funnels to the rails below to keep the engine's drivers from slipping. Photo by Bill Blewett.

OPPOSITE: Here are two views of 2-6-2 #7, the second locomotive purchased from Maui's Kahului Railroad in September of 1937. Victor Norton caught her sitting with sister #2 behind the enginehouse. Bill Blewett had better luck on this visit, finding #7 working a train of cane cars in the mill yard. Except for the trailing truck, #7 was quite similar to #2, both having 40-inch drivers, 12x18-inch cylinders and weighing 28 tons. Photo above by Victor Norton, Jr., Hawaiian Railway Society Collection; Photo below by Bill Blewett.

BELOW: Here's #7 again, this time double-headed with what appears to be 0-6-2T #5. Note the sand car that was placed between the two locomotives in order to help control slipping drivers on the lighter tank locomotive. Photo by Bill Blewett.

BOTTOM: These are a few pieces of Waialua Agricultural Company's non-revenue equipment. The cars behind the flat and tank cars are the plantation's "passenger cars" that carry workers from company housing near the mill to their worksites in remote fields. Photo by Bill Blewett.

TOP: Here is the first of four Waialua Agricultural's locomotives that both Victor Norton and Bill Blewett missed. Fortunately Vitaly Uzoff found them, and Victor then obtained prints for his album. 0-6-0T #1 was WACO's first locomotive, built by Baldwin Locomotive Works in Philadelphia. Both photos by Vitaly V. Uzoff; Victor Norton, Jr. Coll.

ABOVE: WACO #4 was built two years after #1 and #2, but by then the preferred wheel arrangement for Hawaii's plantation locomotives had become the 0-6-2T like #4 shown here. Thirty-three inch wheels were common to both types, but the newer, larger locomotives were built with 11x16-inch cylinders, versus the previous 9x16-inch.

OPPOSITE ABOVE: This is WACO #6, the little locomotive that is linked so closely with the establishment of the Hawaiian Railway Society. This 25-ton 0-6-2T is believed to be the only locomotive ever built in the Hawaiian Islands, having been assembled in 1919 in Waialua Agricultural Company's shops from spare parts, plus a new boiler from Baldwin. After Waialua Agricultural eliminated their plantation railway system in 1952, WACO #6 was put on display in a park adjacent to their sugar mill, where she sat until 1971. Then, in a sadly deteriorated condition, she was donated to the fledgling Hawaiian Railway Society as their first acquisition. Moved to the Navy's railway facility at Naval Ammunition Depot Lualualei, society members rebuilt WACO #6 to operating condition. She now sits as a static display at the HRS museum in Ewa, although an ongoing fund drive effort envisions bringing her back to life. Photo by Vitaly V. Uzoff, Collection of Victor Norton, Jr.

OPPOSITE BELOW: Here is a nice action shot of #5 out on the main line with a load of cane cars. Photo by Vitaly V. Uzoff, Collection of Victor Norton, Jr.

ABOVE: Finally, a nice view of a plantation diesel locomotive. Not much is known about #9. It is a Plymouth diesel-mechanical locomotive that Waialua Agricultural purchased in the early 1940's. Many plantations purchased a small internal combustion locomotive to work around the yard and shops in the off-season, noting that a diesel could be started and put to work at almost a moment's notice, versus warming up the heavy fuel and a steam locomotive's boiler for hours and hours before it could be put into service. Photo by Vitaly V. Uzoff, Collection of Victor Norton, Jr.

GRANT OAKES COLLECTION

BELOW: As mentioned in the introduction, we really do not know as much about Grant Oakes as some of Hawaii's other railfan photographers. We do know that he was in the Army on Oahu during the summer of 1942, and from his donated negative collection, we can tell that he visited both the OR&L in Honolulu and the Waialua Agricultural plantation during that time. Shown here are the best of his photographs from what obviously was a fun-filled and productive day. This first view shows WACO #2, the 2-6-0 purchased from Maui's Kahului Railroad in 1937, taking on water at the enginehouse. Photo by Grant Oakes, Jr., Hawaiian Railway Society Collection.

OPPOSITE ABOVE: Number 2 was soon back at work, putting together a train of empty Fricke chain side cane cars. In the patriotic spirit of 1942, someone has chalked "VICTORY" on #2's toolbox. Photo by Grant Oakes, Jr., Hawaiian Railway Society Collection.

OPPOSITE BELOW: Here is a tender view of #2 working the mill yard. Note the offset headlight on the tender, with the lens painted black in accordance with Territorial regulations imposed during the first days after the attack on Pearl Harbor. Photo by Grant Oakes, Jr., Hawaiian Railway Society Collection.

ABOVE: Grant also found 0-6-2T #5 under steam that day, and he took the nicely lighted front-3/4 view above and this close-up of the cab. Heavy fuel oil was carried in the tank behind the cab, and water in the saddle-tank over the boiler. Both photos by Grant Oakes, Jr., Hawaiian Railway Society Collection.

BELOW: The long strings of small cane cars heaped to overflowing with cane stalks must have been quite an unusual sight to the visiting servicemen, because almost every one of them took a photograph similar to this one. Both photos this page by Grant Oakes, Jr., Hawaiian Railway Society Collection.

BOTTOM: Film was scarce during the War, so many railfans confined their photography to locomotives. However, these next several photographs show that Grant Oakes really did a nice job capturing the often overlooked plantation cars. The first of these is a Fricke chain side cane car. Waialua Agricultural employed almost seven hundred of these cars. The chains would be deployed as shown here for loading, but once the loaded car reached the mill the four rings, one on each end of each side, would be lifted from their posts and the chains dropped out of the way, so that the cane stalks could be pushed off the car and onto a conveyor into the mill.

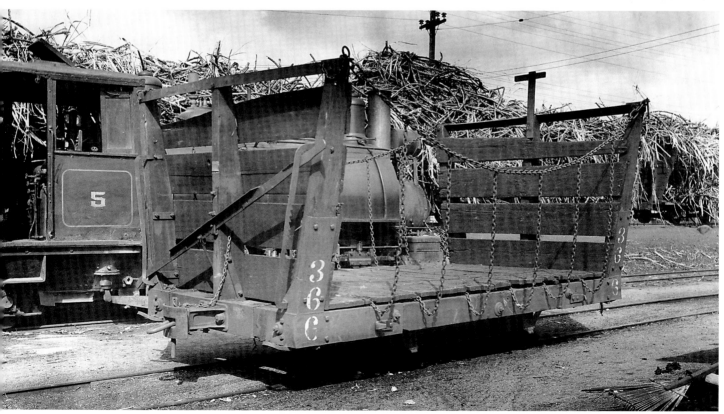

BELOW: Many older cane cars were converted for non-revenue use. Gregg flare side door cane cars were used prior to the Fricke cars, and #7 and #8 shown here appear to have been converted from the plantation's earlier fleet of cars.

BOTTOM: Here is another converted cane car -- this one has been turned into a sand car similar to the one shown earlier. Both photos this page by Grant Oakes, Jr., Hawaiian Railway Society Collection.

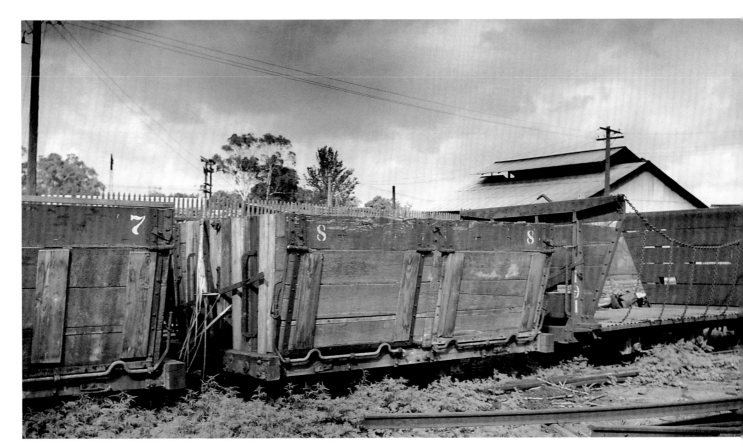

TOP: This one is rather unusual -- a poison car, presumably for hauling weed killer to the field laborers who would apply it by hand wherever required. Both photos this page by Grant Oakes, Jr., Hawaiian Railway Society Collection.

ABOVE: This is another strange tank car. The tank appears to be a pressure vessel. Could one of the hoses be a steam line to heat up the contents -- perhaps molasses for fertilizer or heavy oil for fuel?

TOP: This end view of a Fricke cane car shows the brake system used on cane cars. Plantation locomotives and cars had only hand brakes. Those on the cars were applied using the big lever on one end of the car. Because of the roughness of the track sections, ordinary knuckle couplers could not be used. Instead, the cars were connected by a steel link between removable pins on each car.

ABOVE: In addition to photographing the trains around the mill, Grant obviously got a cab ride. Unfortunately the name of the engineer is not known. Both photos this page by Grant Oakes, Jr., Hawaiian Railway Society Collection.

BELOW: Here is Grant's view back over the tender of WACO #2, looking at a loaded cane car. Both photos this page by Grant Oakes, Jr., Hawaiian Railway Society Collection.

BOTTOM: Grant's final view shows WACO #2 sitting outside the plant on the OR&L interchange track. His railfan adventure must have provided a welcome break from Army combat training prior to shipping out for the campaign to regain possession of the Pacific islands lost during the initial stages of WWII.

Kahuku Plantation Co., Kahuku -- 36" Gauge

ABOVE: What a beautiful photograph! This is Kahuku Plantation #3, an 0-6-2T built by Baldwin in 1905, sitting in front of the Kahuku Mill between assignments. Appearing almost identical to sister #4, she had 33-inch driving wheels and 10x16-inch cylinders. Photo by Bill Blewett.

Kahuku Plantation was another collaborative effort whose founders included James Campbell and Benjamin F. Dillingham. It was formed in 1890, and shortly thereafter ordered equipment for a plantation railway, including an 0-4-2T locomotive from Philadelphia's Baldwin Locomotive Works. A second locomotive, quite similar to the first, was ordered from Baldwin a year later. The OR&L finally arrived in Kahuku, the end of its seventy-mile main line, on the 28th of December 1898, and the plantation expanded enough to purchase one more locomotive in 1905. Not much more is known about the early history of the plantation's railway, that is until 1931. In that year the Kahuku Plantation bought the assets of neighboring Laie Plantation and the Koolau Agricultural Company, plus Oahu's other common carrier railroad -- the Koolau Railway Company, which had served both of those firms and connected with the OR&L in Kahuku. From that time on, what had been the Koolau Railway was operated as an integral part of the Kahuku Plantation's railway. In 1931, the Kahuku

Plantation owned 31 miles of permanent track (including the eleven miles from the Koolau Railway), 2.73 miles of portable track, four steam locomotives and roughly 300 sugar cane and non-revenue cars.

In 1944, the Kahuku Plantation purchased an excess steam locomotive from the Honolulu Plantation Company, but after WWII, when surplus military locomotives became available, Kahuku dieselized its railway operations and retired its last steam locomotive in 1950. Their plantation railway lasted until the end of 1954, longer than any other on Oahu and third only to Grove Farm's and Lihue Plantation's on Kauai, which remained in service until 1957 and 1959 respectively.

Because of its distance from Honolulu, Kahuku Plantation was the most difficult for our servicemen/railfans to reach. Victor Norton never visited the mill, and Bill Blewett came away with only one photograph of a Kahuku locomotive. Fortunately Kent Cochrane spent enough time there to photograph most of their roster, and Victor again obtained copies of Kent's photographs for his collection.

No.	Name	Type	Builder & No.	Year	Notes
					Kahuku Plantation Co., Kahuku -- 36" Gauge Locomotive Roster in 1945:
1	*Keana*	0-4-2T	Baldwin #10756	Mar 1890	Currently at RC&BT RR in Felton, CA
2	*Waimea*	0-6-2T	Baldwin #17687	Apr 1900	Formerly Honolulu Plant. #2, purchased 1944
3	*Kaipapau*	0-6-2T	Baldwin #25742	May 1905	
4	---	0-6-2T	Baldwin #31287	Jul 1907	Formerly Koolau Rwy #1, obtained July 1931

ABOVE: This and the next two photographs were taken by Kent Cochrane in 1946. Number 1 was an 0-4-2T built by Baldwin in 1890 shortly after Kahuku Plantation was founded. The locomotive escaped the scrappers, having been sold to Cliff House Properties in 1950, and then to Roaring Camp and Big Trees in 1966, where she remains -- and sometimes runs -- today. Photograph by Kent Cochrane, Collection of Victor Norton, Jr.

BELOW: This is yet another excellent photograph by Kent Cochrane. Here we see numbers 2 and 3 undergoing repairs in Kahuku Plantation's enginehouse, while a shop mechanic waits motionless for Kent's time exposure to end. In this view 0-6-2T #3, Baldwin 1905, sits on the left, while her older cousin, 0-6-2T (third) #2, built by Baldwin for Honolulu Plantation in 1900, sits on the right. Note the small tanks on either side of #2's smokebox -- these carried extra sand to provide traction for the locomotive's driving wheels. Photograph by Kent Cochrane, Collection of Victor Norton, Jr.

OPPOSITE ABOVE: 0-6-2T #4, one of two locomotives obtained as part of the Koolau Railway purchase in 1931, was built by Baldwin in 1907. She is shown sitting outside Kahuku's enginehouse on a beautiful Hawaiian day. Photograph by Kent Cochrane, Collection of Victor Norton, Jr.

OPPOSITE BELOW: This is Victor Norton's only view of the Kahuku Plantation Company's railway system. His album caption describes this as a bridge near Laie. Laie was a settlement founded by the Mormons on Oahu's Windward Coast, 2.5 miles from Kahuku, and it was served by the Koolau Railway, Oahu's second common carrier railroad, from the line's inception in 1905 until that line was purchased by the Kahuku Plantation Company in July 1931. The Koolau Railway originally ran eleven miles in a southeasterly direction from Kahuku to Kahana, and it provided both passenger and freight service along this section of the coast throughout its relatively brief life. Shortly after taking over the Koolau Railway, the Kahuku Plantation Company removed the furthest two miles of track, so that the village of Punaluu became the end of its line. Photo by Victor Norton, Jr., Hawaiian Railway Society Collection.

ABOVE: Bill Blewett's view of Waimanalo Sugar Company #1 gives the appearance of a railway that has shut down for the off-season, but is ready to resume operations for the next harvest. However, it is likely that this little 0-4-2T has turned its last wheel under its own power. The little side-stake cane cars had a capacity of three tons. Photo by Bill Blewett.

The Waimanalo Sugar Company, the easternmost sugar plantation on Oahu, was chartered in 1880. Their plantation railway system was begun in that year, but because the new locomotive from Baldwin had not yet arrived, their first crop, in January of 1881, was hauled to the mill by teams of mules pulling the railway's small two-ton cane cars. Waimanalo's first locomotive, an eight-ton 0-4-2T originally named *Thos. Cummins* after the plantation's founder, arrived in May. Like all plantations, acquisition of steam locomotives made an immediate improvement in Waimanalo Sugar Company's productivity which allowed the plantation to expand. Like several other early railroads in the Kingdom of Hawaii, Hawaii's King Kalakaua was an early and frequent rider of the little line, visiting at least three times in the 1882-1883 timeframe. During that same period expansions were made to the mill, the railroad and the steamboat pier where raw sugar was shipped to Honolulu.

Two more 0-4-2T locomotives, quite similar to the first one, were purchased from Baldwin over the next several years, so that according to Jesse Conde's *Sugar Trains*, the 1931 Gilmore's *Hawaiian Sugar Manual* described the Waimanalo Sugar Company as having seven miles of permanent track and three miles of portable track, 207 side-stake three-ton cane cars and three eight-ton locomotives. A fourth very similar locomotive would be purchased from the Kaiwiki Sugar Company on the island of Hawaii in 1941.

You may wonder why the Waimanalo Sugar Company stuck with little eight-ton locomotives while almost all of the other plantations progressed to fifteen and then twenty-five or even thirty-five-ton locomotives. Their problem concerned the soil conditions of their fields. Oahu's eastern, "Windward," coast is where the prevailing tradewinds first hit the island, and being blocked by the Koolau mountain range, dump copious amounts of rainfall on the property. Irrigation was never an issue then, but the soil did not drain well, and became quite muddy -- making it very difficult for

No.	Name	Type	Builder & No.	Year	Notes
\multicolumn{6}{l}{Waimanalo Sugar Co., Waimanalo -- 36" Gauge Locomotive Roster in 1945:}					
1	*Nalo*	0-4-2T	Baldwin #5287	Sept 1880	Originally named *Thos. Cummins*
2	*Pokaa*	0-4-2T	Baldwin #30340	Feb 1907	Originally #3; Now at Grizzly Flats RR in California
3	*Olomana*	0-4-2T	Baldwin #6753	May 1883	Originally #2; Now at RR Museum of PA
4	---	0-4-2T	Baldwin #11900	May 1891	Purchased from Kaiwiki Sugar Co. in May 1941; Reported to be undergoing restoration in California

mules or tractors to pull loaded cane cars over portable track as was done at the other plantations. Waimanalo was unique in that they were the only plantation that ran their locomotives on portable track. Hence the need for very light locomotives, which were used right up to the end of the plantation's railway operations in 1944, when trucks that could drive directly from the fields to the mill were used. Unfortunately, the mud problem that affected the mules also affected the trucks, and the Waimanalo Sugar Company was liquidated in 1947. On the positive side though, three of their four locomotives were saved -- two moved to Ward Kimble's (private) Grizzly Flats RR in California, while the third also survived to go to California, but its current status is not known.

In spite of the fact that the Waimanalo Sugar Company ended its rail operations well before the end of the War, several of our railfan servicemen visited the plantation and came away with interesting views of this unique property. Bill Blewett visited early enough -- probably in late 1944 or early 1945 -- that his photographs show a railway system shut down but appearing ready to resume operations at the beginning of the next harvest season. Victor Norton visited approximately one year later and found locomotives #1 and #2 almost hidden by the fast-growing vegetation. Kent Cochrane must have visited after that and found the four locomotives in open storage.

ABOVE: Here is a closer look at Waimanalo Sugar #1, this time with Bill Blewett in the cab. This photo gives a better view of Waimanalo's side-stake cane cars and the simplicity of their little locomotives. The vines on the smokebox and cab indicate that #1 may not have been active for quite a while. Collection of Bill Blewett, Photographer unknown.

OPPOSITE ABOVE: By the time Victor Norton reached Waimanalo -- probably early in 1946 -- numbers 2 and 1 had been moved to a siding and the then wild-growing sugar cane had taken its revenge. Number 2 was another 0-4-2T and, having been built in 1907, was the newest of Waimanalo's locomotives. Photo by Victor Norton, Jr., Hawaiian Railway Society Collection.

OPPOSITE BELOW: This is the first of three photographs of Waimanalo Sugar Company locomotives that Victor Norton bought from Kent Cochrane after the War. These three 0-4-2T locomotives were built by Baldwin Locomotive Works between 1883 and 1907. This is #2, which was originally built for Waimanalo Sugar in 1907 as their number 3 and named *Pokaa*. (Since #2 is sitting with #1, I wonder if Kent chopped down the offending sugar cane that had blocked Victor's view to get this shot?) *Pokaa* was purchased by Gerald M. Best, author of *Railroads of Hawaii*, in 1948, and later sold to Disney animator Ward Kimball for his Grizzly Flats Railroad in San Gabriel, California, where, renamed *Chloe*, she remains operational today. Photograph by Kent Cochrane, Collection of Victor Norton, Jr.

ABOVE: This is #3, built for Waimanalo Sugar in 1883 as their #2. She was originally named *Puaalii*, and was later renamed *Olomana*. Like #2, this little 0-4-2T was purchased by Gerry Best in 1948, and for many years she also operated on Ward Kimball's Grizzly Flats Railroad. However, even bigger things were in store for *Olomana*. In 1977 Gerry Best donated her to the Smithsonian Museum in Washington, DC, and now the beautifully restored little locomotive can be found on loan and displayed at the Railroad Museum of Pennsylvania at Strasburg, Pennsylvania. Photograph by Kent Cochrane, Collection of Victor Norton, Jr.

BELOW: Waimanalo #4 was built by Baldwin in 1891 for the Kaiwiki Sugar Company at Ookala -- located on the northeastern coast of the Big Island of Hawaii -- as their #1, named *Doctor*. When Kawiki Sugar abandoned its railway system in 1939, the little 0-4-2T became excess and almost assuredly should have been scrapped as an obsolete design. However, being almost identical to Waimanalo Sugar's three locomotives, she found a new home with them in 1941 as their #4. Waimanalo Sugar Company's equipment was offered for sale when the plantation was abandoned, and little #4 was purchased and taken to California for restoration; however, she seems to have disappeared, and her current status is not known. Photograph by Kent Cochrane, Collection of Victor Norton, Jr.

BIBLIOGRAPHY

Best, Gerald M., *Railroads of Hawaii*, San Marino: Golden West Books, 1978

Bonnell, Henry F., *Hawaiian Rails of Yesteryear*, Ewa: The Hawaiian Railway Society, 1997

Chiddix, Jim and Simpson, MacKinnon, *Next Stop Honolulu! The Story of the Oahu Railway and Land Company*, Honolulu: Sugar Cane Press, 2004

Conde, Jesse C., *Fowler Locomotives in the Kingdom of Hawaii*, Peterborough: Narrow Gauge Railway Society, 1994

Conde, Jesse C., *Sugar Trains Pictorial*, Felton: Glenwood Publishers, 1975

Conde, Jesse C. and Best, Gerald M., *Sugar Trains*, Felton: Glenwood Publishers, 1973

Hilton, George W., *American Narrow Gauge Railroads*, Chicago: Stanford University Press, 1994

Hungerford, John B., *Hawaiian Railroads*, Reseda: Hungerford Press, 1963

Morrison, Boone, "Bringing the Baldwins Home," *Narrow Gauge and Shortline Gazette*, Vol. 30, No. 4 (September/October, 2004), pp. 60-63

Treiber, Gale E., *Hawaiian Railway Album, Vol. 2 -- Along the Main Lines of the Oahu Railway and Land Co. and the Hawaii Consolidated Railway*, Hanover, PA: The Railroad Press, 2005

Treiber, Gale E., "Oahu's Railways Since WWII," *The Railroad Press*, Issue No. 66 (July/August/September, 2005), pp. 10-29